Singing with Joy

MAJESTIC ANTHEMS FOR FESTIVAL CHOIR

Shout with joy before
the Lord, O earth!
Obey him gladly;
come before him,
singing with joy.
(Psalm 100:1-2, TLB)

Don Marsh

ALLEGIS® PUBLICATIONS
Kansas City, MO 64141

CONTENTS

God Reigns

Jesus Shall Reign
Our God Reigns

Arranged by Don Marsh

Brightly ♩ = ca. 134

15
e'er the sun Does his suc - ces - sive
G/D D sus D 15 A/C♯ B m B m9
Divisi
19
jour - neys run; His king - dom
Divisi
E m7 G M7 A sus A 19 F♯ F♯sus/G♯ F♯7/A♯
spread from shore to shore,
B m D2/A G D/F♯ A7/E D A/C♯ A sus/B A A/G

*Words and Music by Leonard E. Smith, Jr. © 1974, 1978 by L. E. Smith/New Jerusalem Music, Box 225, Clarksboro, NJ 08020. All rights reserved. Used by permission.

moun - tains are the feet of him
Who brings good
Unison mf
F/B♭
E♭/B♭
B♭sus
B♭
Cm/B♭
B♭
35
Divisi
news, good news
C/B♭
F/A
F9
B♭2
B♭
mf
39
An - nounc - ing peace, pro - claim - ing news of
God loves us so– see here His hands, His
Divisi mf
B♭
B♭sus/C
B♭/D
E♭
F
Gm/F
F
mf

43
hap - pi - ness: Our God reigns;
feet, His side. Yes, we know
E♭/B♭ B♭ E♭/G Gm7 43 Cm7 Cm7/E♭
CD: 4 1st time
CD: 6 2nd time
cresc.
our God reigns! Our God
He's a - live!
f
F E♭/F B♭ Cm/B♭ B♭ Fm/D
47
reigns! Our God reigns!
E♭ E♭/F Dm/F F7 B♭ Cm/B♭ B♭ Cm7

CD: 5
1st time
2nd time to Coda
(to pg. 11, meas. 62)
51
Our God reigns!
Our God
B♭/D D+ D7 E♭2 Cm7 F E♭/F
reigns!
Unison mf
Out from the tomb He
55
B♭ Cm/B♭ B♭7 E♭M7
decresc.
mf
came with grace and maj - es - ty.
He is a -
F/E♭ E♭M7 F/E♭ E♭/G F/A B♭ Cm/B♭ B♭

59
D.S. al Coda
(to pg. 8, meas. 38)
live, a - live!
live! He is a - live!
Cm9
F/C
F9sus
B♭
Fsus/B♭
B♭sus/F
CODA
cresc.
CD: 7
reigns!
B♭
B♭sus
B♭/A♭
G sus
G
G sus/A
G2/B

67
A few voices
f
Je - sus shall
ff rit.
a tempo
Our God reigns!
G2/B G/B C Gm/E F FM7 F
rit. ff
a tempo
reign wher - e'er the sun;
Our God reigns! Our God
F/G Em/G G7 Am Dm/A C/G Dm/F C/E E+ E7

71
His jour - neys run. Our God reigns, He shall
Je - sus shall
reigns!
Our God reigns; He shall
F2 Dm7 G F/G C C4/2
75
reign.
reign.
Je - sus shall reign!
reign.
C C4/2 C F/C G/C F/C G/C

79
Our God reigns! Ev - ery crea - ture
FM7 G Ab/C Bb2/C
rise and sing! Our God reigns!
rit.
AbM7/C Bb/C Gm7 C C/F
Je - sus reigns!
C/F BbM7 Gm7 N.C. C
8va
8vb

Bless the Lord

Adapted from Psalm 103
by DON MARSH

DON MARSH
Arranged by Don Marsh

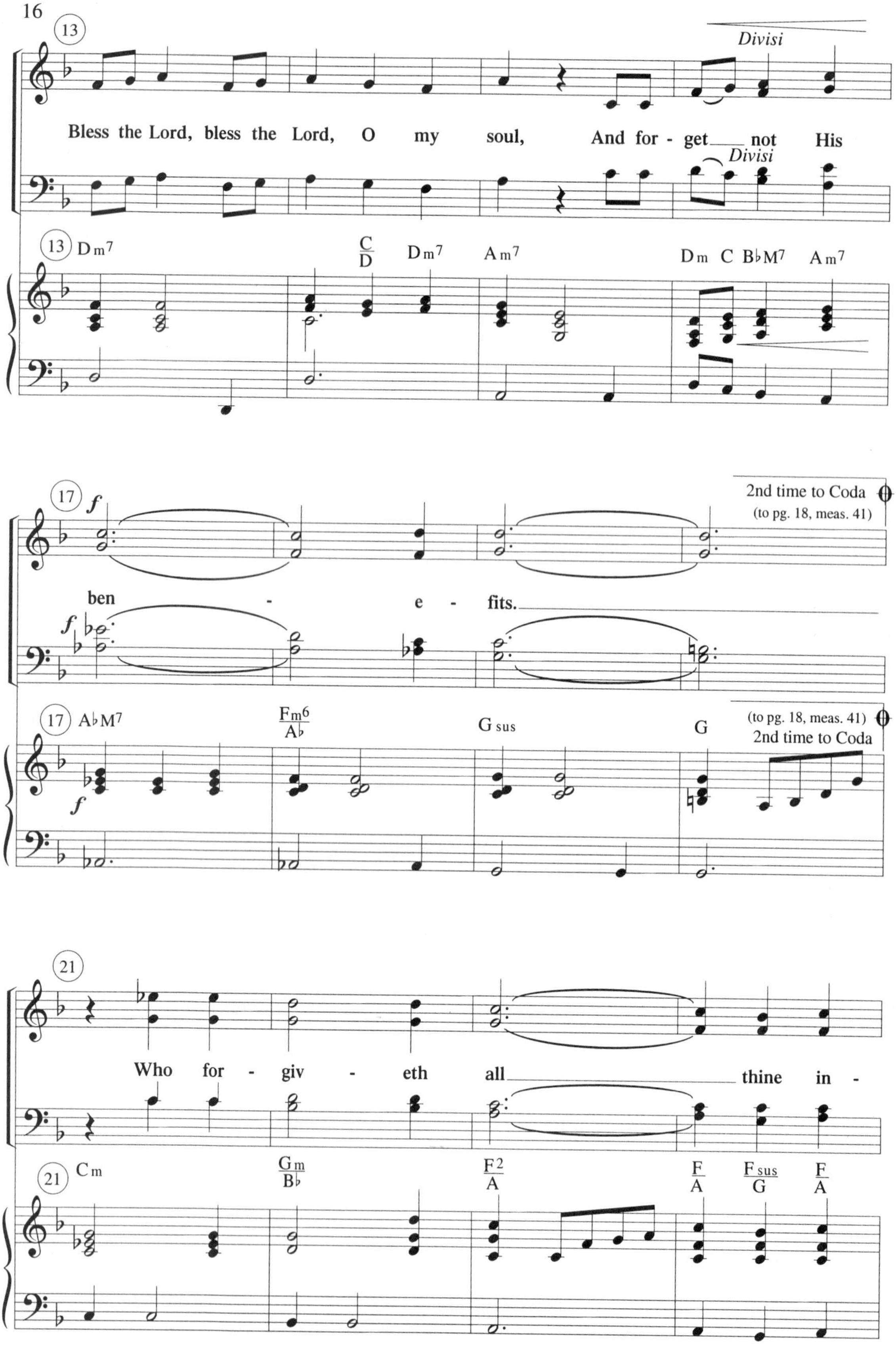
13
Divisi
Bless the Lord, bless the Lord, O my soul, And for - get not His
Divisi
Dm7 C/D Dm7 Am7 Dm C B♭M7 Am7
17
f
2nd time to Coda
(to pg. 18, meas. 41)
ben - e - fits.
A♭M7 Fm6/A♭ Gsus G
21
Who for - giv - eth all thine in -
Cm Gm/B♭ F2/A F/A Fsus/G F/A

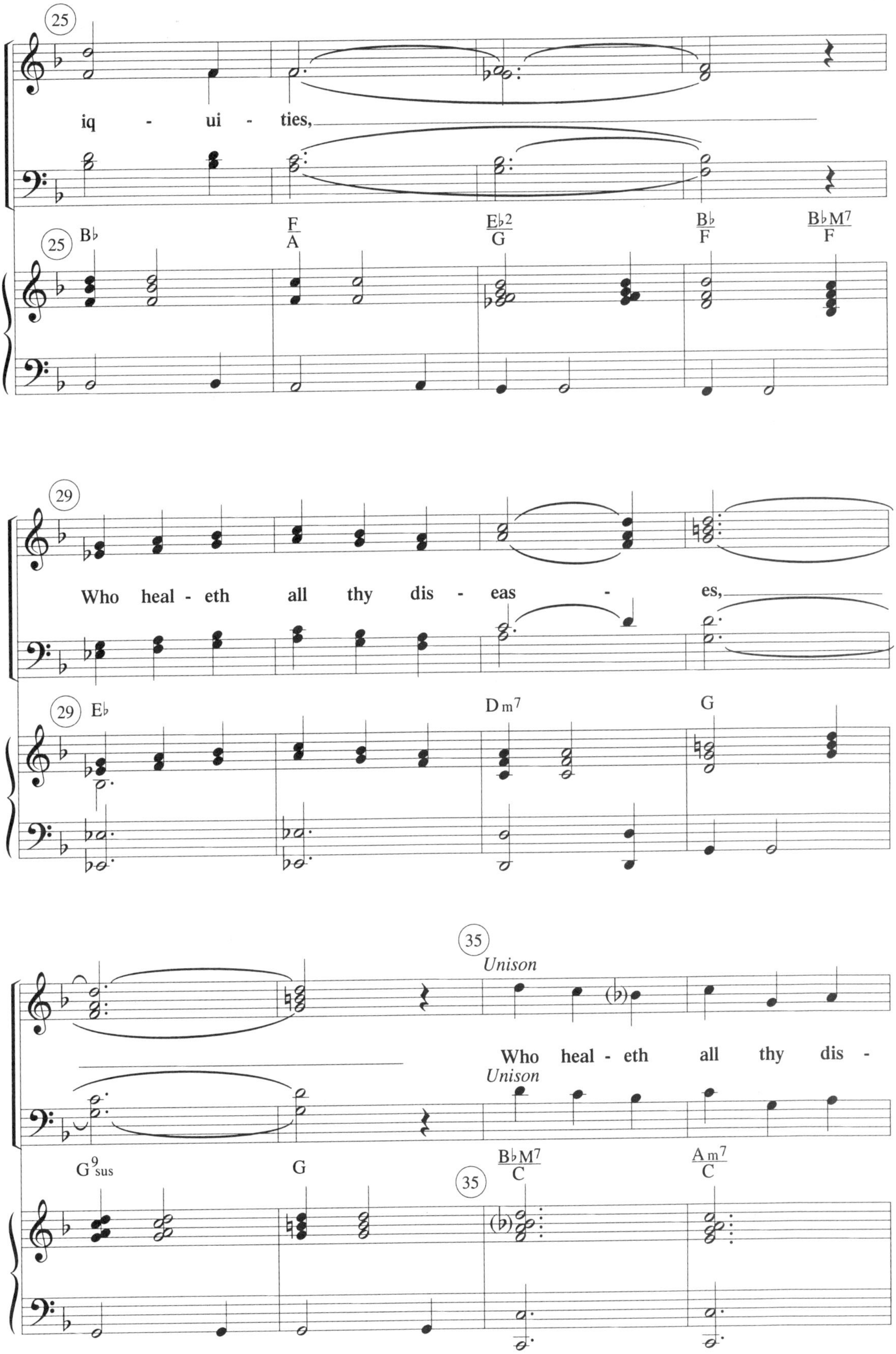
25
iq - ui - ties,
B♭
F/A
E♭2/G
B♭/F
B♭M7/F
29
Who heal - eth all thy dis - eas - es,
E♭
Dm7
G
35
Unison
Who heal - eth all thy dis -
Unison
G9sus
G
B♭M7/C
Am7/C

D.S. al Coda
(to pg. 15, meas. 5)
eas - es.
Gm7 B♭M7 C2 C C2 C Gm9 Am7 B♭M7
D.S. al Coda
(to pg. 15, meas. 5)
CODA
CD: 9
43
CODA
Cm7 Dsus D G2 C/D D
46
Unison mf
Who re - deem - eth thy life
Dsus G2 G F/G
mf

49
from de - struc - tion,
49
F/G
G
E♭M7/G
E♭M7/D
54
Who crown - eth thee with lov -
Fm7/G
Gm7
Gm7/D
54
G2
G
C/G
58
- ing - kind - ness
G
58
D/F♯
Dsus/E
D

cresc.
62
Divisi
And with ten - der mer -
cresc.
Dsus D
C
D/C
C
cresc.
f
66
cies. Who sat - is - fies thy mouth
f
Divisi
D/C
E♭/B♭
E♭2/B♭
A♭/B♭
f
69
72
mf
with good things, So that thy
mf
A♭/B♭
B♭
Gm7
Cm
mf

76
CD: 10
youth is re - newed like the ea -
Cm/E♭
Gm
76 C sus
80 Unison
gle's.
Bless the Lord, bless the
Unison
C
C2 C
B♭2/C
80 F2
84
Lord, O my soul;
And all that is with - in
F2
F sus 84 B♭M7

88
me,
Bless His ho - ly name.
Bless the Lord, bless the
B♭M7
B♭M9
F2/A
B♭M7
B♭/C
88
Dm7
Divisi
92
f
Lord, O my soul,
And for - get not His ben -
Divisi
f
Dm7
C/D
Dm7
Am7
Dm
C
B♭M7
Am7
92
A♭M7
f
CD: 11
- e - fits.
Fm6/A♭
G sus
G
G sus/F
G/F

99
mf
Bless the Lord,
mf
C/E
D
99
G2
mf
103
Bless Him, ye an - gels; Bless the Lord,
G
A♭/G
Gm7
A♭/G
103
107
All ye, His hosts; Bless the Lord,
A♭/G
Gm7
A♭M7/G
Gm7
107
C

111
CD: 12
All His works praise Him! Bless the Lord, O my
C
Db/C
Cm7
Db/C
Db/G
D/C
G/B
Gsus/A
G
soul!
115
Unison
Bless the Lord, bless the Lord, O my
Dsus
D
D/F#
G2
CM7/D
D7
C/D
119
soul; And all that is with - in me,
Bless His
GM7
G
C/G
CM9

123
ho - ly name. Bless the Lord, bless the Lord, O my
Am7/4 G2/B CM7 C/D 123 Em7 D/E Em7
Divisi 127
soul, And for - get not His ben - e -
Divisi
Bm7 Em D CM7 Bm7 127 B♭M7 Gm6/B♭
131
fits. Bless the Lord, bless the
A sus A 131 Dm C/D Dm/C C

135
Lord!
Bless the Lord, bless the
B♭M7
Am7
B♭M7
C2
135
Dm
139
Lord,
O my soul.
B♭M7
G
139
D
DM7
G
A
D
C
D
D
DM7
G
A
D
C
D
D
8va
8vb

Light of the World

Adapted from Scripture
by DON MARSH

DON MARSH
Arranged by Don Marsh

Moderate, with feeling ♩ = ca. 80

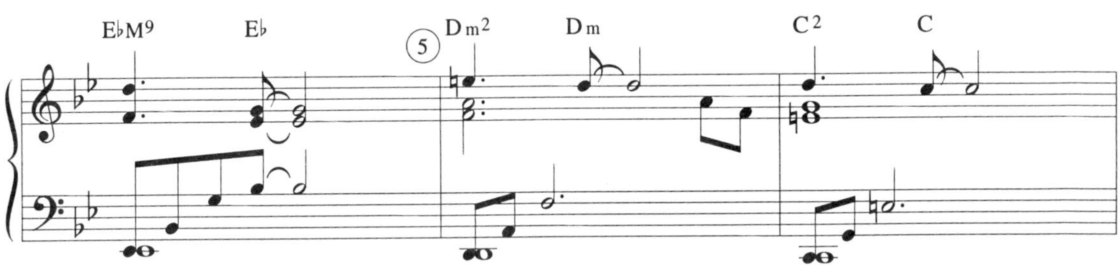

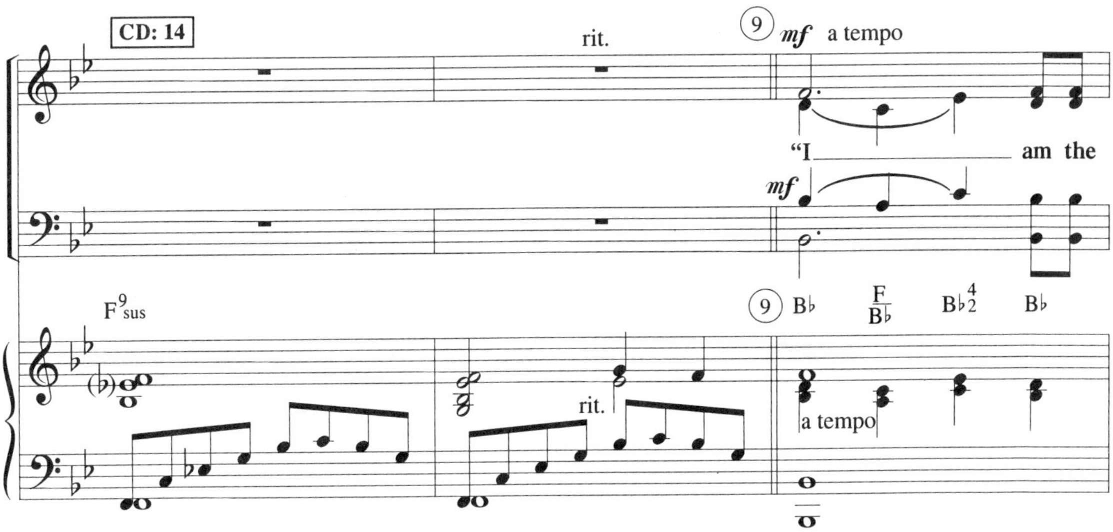

Unison
Light of the world." Who -
Unison
A♭2 B♭/A♭ A♭M7 B♭ F/B♭ B♭4/2 B♭ F/A E♭2/G B♭/F
13
ev - er fol - lows Me shall not walk in dark - ness,
E♭M7 F/E♭ Dm7 B♭/D C4/2 Cm E♭M7/A♭ A♭2 E♭/G
16
cresc.
Divisi
f
mf
But shall have the Light of Life! The
D/F♯ Dsus/E D/F♯ Gm F/A B♭

peo - ple liv - ing in the dark - ness in the
F♯+ G 4 2 Gm F/E♭ E♭
mf
20
sha - dow of death, Have seen a great
cresc.
E° A7/E Dm2/F Dm/F D/F♯ Gm F
f
light, They have seen a great light!
24
CD: 15
ff
E♭ Dm7 Cm7 F Dm7 G2 G
3

Unison
mf
28
When you walk in the
G2
C2/G
G2
mf
Light, The blood of Je - sus, God's
C2/G
D/G
G
D/G
C2/G
32
Divisi
Son pur - i - fies you from sin.
Unison
G
G4/2
G
CM9
C
D2/F♯
D/F♯
F♯m7

36
The dark - ness is past, The
mf
Dm2/F Dm/F C2/E CM7 Am7 G2/B G2/F
Divisi
Unison
f
40
true Light now shines. Be - lieve and put your trust in Him
C2/E Am G Em7 Am Am2
That you may be - come the sons of God.
Em/G Gm Gm2

45
CD: 16
Dm
Dm2
Dm
C2
C
F2
mf
D♭M7/F
E♭/F
F2
D♭M7/F
D♭6/F
There shall be a new heav - en,
mf
Unison
mf
51
and a new earth,
There shall be no night
Divisi
Unison
F2
F2/E♭
D♭
B♭m7
E♭/B♭
B♭m

there, Nor the light of the sun. For the
F2/A D♭/A♭ Fm7/A♭ B♭m/A♭ C sus C
Divisi
glo-ry of God lights the ci-ty, And the saved shall walk in the
Divisi
Dm C/D Dm B♭M7 Am7 Dm C/D
Light. And the kings of the earth, Bring their
Unison
Unison
Dm B♭M7 C Dm C/D B♭/D Am/D

glo - ry and hon - or.
hon - or, and He shall reign, Reign for -
Divisi
A♭ A♭2 A♭ G sus F 9 6
64
Divisi cresc.
ev - er! He shall reign, for -
cresc.
G 4 2 G F/G G
CD: 17
rit.
69
Broadly
a tempo
ev - er! "I am the
G G 9 sus C G/C C 4 2 C
rit.
a tempo

Light of the world." Who -
B♭2 B♭M9 C/B♭ B♭M7 C G/C C 4/2 C G2/B F2/A C/G
73
ev - er fol - lows Me shall not walk in dark - ness,
FM7 G/F Em7 C/E D 4/2 Dm Am/D FM7 G
But shall have the Light of Life!
E/G♯ Esus/F♯ E/G♯ Am G/B C C/E Csus/D C

77
But shall have the Light of Life! Light of
G/B Gsus/A G/B C Bm7 Em Am/E Em
Life! Light of the world!
rit.
81
Eb Eb/D C Gm7 C G D/G G
molto rit.
Light of the world!
F2 Dm7 G G#4 G2 G

I Will Sing

I Will Sing of My Redeemer
I Will Sing the Wondrous Story

Arranged by Don Marsh

deem - er And His won - drous love to
deem - er; His tri - um - phant pow'r I'll
D/E D/B C/E D7/F♯
me; On the cru - el cross He
tell, How the vic - to - ry He
G2 G2/F♯ Em
13
CD: 19 1st time
CD: 21 2nd time
suf - fered, From the curse to set me
giv - eth O - ver sin, and death, and
D/E Am D
12/8

17
f Divisi
free.
hell.
Sing, O sing of my Re-
f Divisi
G G2
17
C
f
deem - er. With His blood He purchased
G
D/F♯
Dsus/E D
21
On the cross
me. On the cross, on the cross He sealed my
G Gsus/A G2/B
21
C C/D

par - don,
Paid the debt and made me
Bm7
Em7
G/B
Bm7 C2
D7
1
free.
CD: 20
mf
free, I'm free.
G2
Gsus
C2
C2/E
(to pg. 37, meas. 9)
Men unison
2. I will
2
CD: 22
free, I'm free.
Dsus
D
G
G9sus

Unison
mf
32
*"I Will Sing the Wondrous Story"
I was lost, but Je - sus
Unison
mf
G
G9sus
C sus
found me, Found the sheep that went a -
C
G7/C
36
stray, Threw His lov - ing arms a -
C
N.C.

CD: 23
round me, Drew me back into His
way. Yes, I'll
Divisi
Divisi
A♭ A♭9sus
41
sing the wondrous sto - ry Of the
D♭ G♭/D♭ D♭M7 G♭/D♭ D♭/F D♭sus/E♭ D♭2 D♭
41

Christ who died for me; Sing it
A♭7sus/D♭
A♭7/C
E♭m/C
D♭
A♭
45
with the saints in glo - ry, Gath - ered
45
B♭m/G
G♭9
Fm7
D♭/F
B♭m7
B♭m/G
CD: 24
cresc.
by the crys - tal sea.
cresc.
A♭
G♭/A♭
A♭
D♭
D♭/C♭
cresc.

Unison ff
50
Yes, I'll sing the won - drous
Unison ff
A sus
A
D
G/D
A/D
G/D
ff
sto - ry Of the Christ who died for
D
A/D
G2
G2/A
G2/B
A2/C♯
Soprano/Tenor
54
Sing it with the saints in
me;
Sing it with the saints in
Alto/Bass
D
Em7
F♯m7
Bm
Bm/A
G
D M7/G
G

glo - ry, Gath - ered by the crys - tal
glo - ry, Gath - ered by the crys - tal
D/F♯ Dsus/E D A/C♯ Bm7 Bm7/G♯ A G/A A
sea.
sea.
Soprano/Alto
Sing with the
Divisi
Tenor/Bass
Divisi
B♭ C2 C2/A
59
saints in glo - ry, Sing with the
Unison
Divisi
Unison
Divisi
59
B♭ C2 C2/A

Unison
saints in glo - ry,
Unison
B♭
C2
C2/A
63
Divisi
Sing of my Re - deem - er!
Divisi
63
D
D/C B♭M7
C2/A
N.C.
D
N.C.
B♭/C C/B♭
D
fff

You Are Holy

Holy, Holy, Holy Is the Lord of Hosts
You Are Holy

Arranged by Don Marsh

With awe ♩ = ca. 84

14
hosts; Ho - ly, ho - ly, ho - ly
C4/2 C C/B 14 Am Am2/G F2 G Am
Divisi
18
is the Lord of hosts. The whole earth is full of His
Divisi
D/F♯ D7/F♯ G F/A G/B 18 C Csus/D C/E
glo - ry, The whole earth is full of His glo - ry, The
F2 F Cm6/E♭ D Dsus/E D/F♯ G2 G Dm6/F

22
whole earth is full of His glo - ry, Ho - ly is the
E
Esus/F♯
E/G♯
Am2
Am
Fm6/A♭
C/G
G
C/G
G9sus
G7
F/G
Lord.
26
CD: 26
C
Csus
C
G/C
F2/C
F/C
*"You Are Holy"
30
1st time: all (parts)
2nd time: ladies
Unison
1. You are ho - ly–
2. I am weak - ness–
E♭2/B♭
E♭/B♭
B♭
B♭
E♭2/B♭

2nd time: add men
34
2nd time: ladies
I come in si - lence. You are
You, Lord, are pow - er; I am
Divisi
Unison
B♭
Cm/B♭
B♭M7
E♭/B♭
Cm
34
2nd time: add men
wise– Lord, I come to hear.
sin– You stoop to my need;
F9sus
F7
F9sus
B♭
B♭M7
38
Both times: parts
Divisi
You are God– I come to o - bey
I am scarred– You wrap me in heal -
Divisi
38
E♭
B♭2/D
B♭/D
B♭/A♭
B♭2/A♭

CD: 27 1st time
CD: 29 2nd time
42
You. You are love– I come to draw
ing; I am lost– and You come to
E♭2/G B♭/G E♭ 42 F7sus/C F9sus
46
near.
me.
Ho - ly, ho - ly,
B♭sus B♭ 46 E♭/B♭
B♭ E♭/B♭ F9/C B♭/D

50
Ho - ly, You are ho - ly.
50
D
D sus/E
D7/F♯
G 4/2
Gm
Gm/E♭
Gm/D
54
Fa - ther, Fa - ther,
54
Cm7
B♭2/D
B♭/D
Dm7
Cm/A
D7
D7/F♯
Gm2
Gm
Gm/F
58
Fa - ther, You are love.
58
E♭
Dm7
Cm7
E♭/F
F7
E♭/B♭

CD: 28
(to pg. 49, meas. 30)
B♭ E♭M7 F4/2 F E♭/F F9sus F7
(to pg. 49, meas. 30)
CD: 30
68 Unison mp
Ho - ly, ho - ly,
Ho - ly, ho - ly,
B♭ Gsus G F/G Em/G F/C
C F/C G9/C C
Divisi
ho - ly,
ho - ly, ho - ly,

72
mf
Unison
Ho - ly, You are ho - ly.
Unison
mf
On - ly You are ho - ly.
E/C
Am/C
E/C
D°/C
Am/C
mf
Divisi
76
f
Fa - ther,
Divisi
f
Am/C
Dm7
C2/E
C/E
Em7
Fa - ther,
rit.
Dm/B
E7
E7/G♯
Am2
Am
Am/G
rit.

81 Slower
mf
Fa - ther, You are love.
mf
81 F Em7 Dm7 F/G G7 F/C
mf Slower
86
You are ho - ly.
C C/B F2/A CM7/G D2/F♯ D/F♯ 86 G9sus G7 C4/2
Csus C C2

Hallowed Be Thy Name

Traditional and DON MARSH
Arranged by Don Marsh

*Pronounce as Hal-low-ed-(d)a

11
Thy king - dom come, Thy will be done,
Give us this day our dai - ly bread,
F Dm7 C C/B♭ F/A C7sus/G C7/G F C7/E
CD: 32 1st time
Hal - low - ed - a be Thy name.
O glo - ry.
F Dm Gm/B♭ C7 F N.C.
1
F Am7 B♭
(to pg. 56, meas. 7)
2
La, la, la, la, la, la, la, la, la, la, la.
B♭ Csus
F C F Dm C

19
CD: 33
La, la, la, la, la, la, la, la, la.
Am7 Dm7 Gm7 B♭M7 C Am7 D N.C.
22
Solo
mf
And for-give us all of our debts,
La, la, la, la, la, la, la, la. Hal-low-ed-a be Thy name;
G D G D Em D G

26
Just as we for - give our debt - ors,
La, la, la, la, la, la, la, la.
G N.C. D G D7 G D7
Hal-low-ed-a be Thy name.
Hal-low-ed-a be Thy name. Hal - le - lu - ia.
30
La, la, la, la, la, la,
G Em Am/C D7 G N.C. G D G

CD: 34
la, la, la, la, la.
La, la, la, la, la, la, la, la, la.
G Em D Bm7 Em7 Am7 CM7 D
Solo
36
For Thine is the king - dom, the
G D/G G D/G G D/G
pow - er and glo - ry, Hal - low - ed - a be Thy name. For -
Hal - low - ed - a be Thy name.
G D/G Em D G N.C. D

40
CD: 35
ev - er and ev - er, for - ev - er and ev - er, Hal - low - ed - a be Thy name.
Hal - low - ed - a be Thy name.
G Am/G G D/G G Am/G G Em Am/C D7 G
For - ev - er.
45
f
Our Fa - ther
N.C. G A♭ E♭

who art in heav - en, Hal - low - ed - a be Thy name. Thy
A♭ E♭ Fm E♭ A♭ Fm7 E♭ E♭/D♭
49
king - dom come, Thy will be done, Hal - low - ed - a be Thy name.
A♭/C E♭7sus/B♭ E♭7/B♭ A♭ E♭7/G A♭ Fm B♭m/D♭ E♭7 A♭
53
CD: 36
Thy king - dom come, Thy will be done,
A♭ Fm7 E♭ A♭/C E♭7sus/B♭ E♭7/B♭ A♭ E♭7/G

57
Hal - low - ed - a be Thy name. Hal - le - lu - ia.
La, la, la, la, la, la,
Ab Fm Bbm/Db Eb7 Ab Fm7 Eb
57
Ab Eb Ab
la, la, la, la, la. La, la, la, la, la, la, la, la, la.
Ab Fm Eb Cm7 Fm7 Bbm7 DbM7 Eb
61
Hal - low - ed - a be Thy, Hal - low - ed - a be Thy,
61
Ab Eb Ab Eb

ff
Hal - low - ed - a be Thy, Thy
A♭ E♭ D♭ E♭
66
name! For - ev - er,
ff O glo - ry, Hal - le - lu - ia!
A♭ Fm7 E♭7sus A♭ Fm7 E♭7sus N.C.
Hal - low - ed be Thy name!
D♭ E♭ A♭
8va
8vb

Mighty to Save

includes

My Faith Looks Up to Thee

KEN BIBLE and
RAY PALMER

DON MARSH and
LOWELL MASON
Arranged by Don Marsh

Slowly ♩ = ca. 92

12
You are the bright-ness of His ho - ly face. And yet You
Dm D4/2 Dm Dm7 G9sus G7
12 Am Am2/G Am/G
came; You came to die for me.
D2/F♯ DM7/F♯ D/F♯ Dm/F C2/E C/E Fm(M7)/D Fm6
16
Now You are ris - en, Name a - bove all
16 Em7 A4/2 Am B♭2 B♭M7 B♭

20
names.
Wor - thy of all hon - or,
You are here a - mong us,
E♭M7 E♭6 E♭ C/E F B♭2 B♭ F/A
CD: 38 1st time
CD: 40 2nd time
Divisi
rit.
24
a tempo
Might-y now to save.
Might-y now to save.
My great Re -
Dm7 G7sus G7 C C/B
deem - er,
I lift my eyes to You,
F/A F C/E Dm Dm/C G/B Gsus/A Fm6/A♭ A♭°7

28
Savior on high!
Lord, in Your
Am D Gsus G G/F C/E F
great compassion, Take my sin, and in Your mercy
cresc.
f
G G7/B C4/2 C Csus/D C/E F Dm7 G Em7 Am Am/G
32
Make all I am
Make
Holy in Your
Am/F♯ B7♯5 B7 Dm6/E E7/G♯ Am Dm F/G G7
36

2nd time to Coda
(to pg. 70, meas. 54)
eyes.
C sus
C
C sus/D
C/E
F
Dm7
G
Em7
Am
CD: 39
A♭
A♭/G
F
F/E♭
D
G sus
G
42
Ladies unison
mf
We are the chil - dren of the Fa - ther,
C2
F2/A
F/A
We have been fash - ioned by Your love and grace.
G/B
B♭M7
A7sus
A7

46
Divisi
And yet we fail; We fail to
Dm7 Em7 D2/F♯ D/F♯ Dm/F C/E
look to You.
50
Lord, in Your good - ness
Fm(M7)/D Fm6/G 50 E7♭9 Am Em/G G/F FM7
Unison
Call us to Your face.
Unison
D.S. al Coda
(to pg. 67, meas. 20)
CODA
CD: 41
B♭2 B♭M7 B♭ E♭M7 E♭6 E♭ D G E A
cresc.

Soprano/Tenor
56
ff
My great Re - deem - er,
Alto/Bass with cong.
My faith looks up to Thee,
A sus A D D/C♯ G2/B G D
I lift my eyes to You, Sav - ior on
Thou Lamb of Cal - va - ry, Sav - ior di -
Em Em/D Em/C♯ A7/C♯ Em7/B A7 D D/B D/A E/G♯ Esus/F♯ E
62
high! Lord, in Your great com - pas - sion,
vine! Now hear me while I pray;
A sus A A/G D2/F♯ D/F♯ D G/D G2/D A/D D4/2 D

66
Take my sin, and in Your mer - cy Make all I
Take all my guilt a - way. O let me
F♯m7 Bm7 G/B G2/E A F♯m7 Bm7 Bm/G♯ C♯7♯5 C♯7♭9
am Ho - ly in Your eyes.
from this day Be whol - ly Thine!
F♯m7 Bm Em7 D/A A7 D Dsus D/A D A/C♯ Bm DM7/A
Choir only
70
Soprano/Alto
Divisi
O let me from this day Be whol - ly
Tenor/Bass
Divisi
Bm/G♯ Dm(M7)/G G9 F♯m7 Bm C C/B A

74
Thine! Make all I am
N.C.
Bm6/C♯ C♯7♯5 C♯7♭9 Em6/F♯ F♯7/A♯ Bm2 Bm
78
ho - ly in Your eyes;
Em7 G/A A7 D
Lord, we are Thine.
(6+)
B♭/C B♭ Am7 Dsus N.C. Am7 D

Sing with Joy

Adapted from Psalm 100
by DON MARSH

DON MARSH
Arranged by Don Marsh

11
Unison
all the earth! Sing, sing with joy!
Unison
F2/D
F2(no 3rd)
11
G2(no 3rd)
F2
Divisi
Praise Him all the earth!
Divisi
G2(no 3rd)
F2
G2
G2/F
16
Sing be - fore the Lord!
16
E♭
Dm7
Cm7

CD: 43
C M7
G 2 (no 3rd)
f
Dsus/C
Csus/D
F M7
22
Unison
f
Divisi
Sing with joy, sing with joy be - fore the
Unison f
Divisi
22
G 2
G sus
G
Lord!
27
Unison
Come be - fore,
Unison
F 2
F
F/E
D m7
27
G 2

Sing with joy!
Divisi
come be - fore Him, sing with joy,
Divisi
G2 Gsus G B♭ B♭/A
32
mf
sing with joy! Try to re - al - ize
mf
E7/G♯ Am Asus Am Em7
32
mf
Unison f
36
what this means, The Lord is
Unison f
F2/A F/A FM7 Dm7 36 G9sus G
f

2nd time to Coda
(to pg. 81, meas. 72)
Divisi
God. The Lord is God.
Divisi
2nd time to Coda
(to pg. 81, meas. 72)
G/C C G/C F9sus F/E♭ D sus D
(♯)
CD: 44
42
Unison
mf
He has made us,
D C/D C M7/D D/C
42
B♭2 B♭
decresc.
mf
we are His peo - ple, the sheep of His pas - ture.
B♭4/2 B♭ F/G Gm7 F/G Gm7 F

46
Divisi
He has made us, we are His peo - ple, the sheep of His pas - ture.
F/E♭ B♭/E♭ F/E♭ B♭/E♭ Dm7 Gm7 F/G
Unison
50
Unison
En - ter in - to His gates with thanks-
Dm7 Gm7 F E♭ B♭/D
giv - ing in your heart.
54 Divisi
In - to His courts with
Divisi
E♭ E♭/F F Gm F E♭2 E♭

praise; And be thank - ful un - to Him For the
B♭2/D B♭/D E♭ Dm7 Cm7 F D/F♯
58
Lord is good; His mer - cy is ev - er -
Unison
Gm F E♭ B♭/D E♭ Cm7 F
Divisi
62
last - ing, And His truth en - dures To
E♭/F F F4/2 F B♭ F/A Gm F/G Gm

66
mf
f
all gen - er - a - tions.
Bless His name, bless His
Cm
E♭M7
F
F/E♭
D m7
sub. mf
name!
ff
Bless His name, bless His name!
D m7
G m7
70
fff
Bless His name, bless His name!
CD: 45
D.S. al Coda
(to pg. 76, meas. 20)
CD: 46
CODA
Divisi
God!
Cm7 Dm7 E♭M7
B♭/A♭
D sus
D

74
Unison
Sing with joy! Sing with joy!
Sing with joy to the
Unison
D D4 2 D G2 F9 6
Divisi
Sing with joy! Sing with joy!
78
Unison
Sing with joy!
Lord all the earth! Sing with
Dsus Eb Dm11 Dsus C G2 B F9 6 G2
Sing with joy!
Divisi
Sing with joy! Sing with joy!
joy to the Lord all the earth!
F9 6 Dsus Eb Dm11 Dsus C Dsus B Dsus G

82
fff
Sing with joy!
fff
Divisi
82
D sus
D
N.C.
fff
Sing with joy!
86
N.C.
Dm11
Dm7
86
G2
G sus/D
G sus
G sus/A
C sus/A
FM7
D sus
D sus/G
D sus/C
D sus/B
G sus/A
G

All That Thrills My Soul

Words and Music by
THORO HARRIS
Arranged by Don Marsh

Divisi
Unison
thou - sand In my bless-ed Lord I see.
FM7 F6 Em7 Dm7 G F/G G7 A♭M7
CD: 48
F2 F B♭2
16
mf
Who can cheer the heart like Je - sus,
B♭ B♭M7 E♭/B♭ E♭2/B♭ E♭/B♭

20
Divisi
By His pres-ence all di - vine? True and ten-der, pure and
Divisi
F/B♭ B♭ E♭/G F/A 20 B♭ B♭9
pre - cious, O how blest to call Him
E♭2 E♭ Gm/E F F7
CD: 49
25
mine!
Love of Christ so free-ly
Unison
B♭ B♭/A♭ G♭ A♭2 A♭ 25 B♭2

giv - en, Grace of God be-yond de - gree,
E♭6 9
F2
B♭2
E♭/F
29
Divisi
CD: 50
Mer - cy high-er than the heav - en,
Deep - er than the deep-est
Oo
Divisi
B♭ B♭M7 B♭7
E♭6 9 Cm7
F7
sea!
33
f
All that thrills my soul is Je - sus;
B♭ E♭/F
cresc.
B♭ F♯° Gm2 D7sus D7 E♭2 D♭7♭5

37
mf
He is more than life to me.
And the fair-est of ten
C9sus C7 F9sus F7 B♭9sus B♭9
decresc.
Unison
thou - sand In my bless-ed Lord I see.
E♭ Dm7 Cm7 F7 B♭
cresc.
41
CD: 51
B♭ C/B♭ D♭/A♭ G♭ C2
ff decresc.

45
Unison f
By the crys- tal, flow- ing riv - er,
C
Gb/C
Ab/C
C2
F6 9/C
With the ran- somed I will sing,
49
And for- ev - er and for -
G2/F
C2/E
Gsus
G
C
C/B
CD: 52
ev - er Praise and glo- ri - fy the King.
Am
Fm
Fm/D
G
G7sus
G7

53
ff
Divisi
All that thrills my soul is Je - sus; He is more than life to
C G♯° Am2 E7sus E7 F2 E♭7♭5 D9sus D7
me. And the fair-est of ten thou - sand
57
G9sus G9 C9sus C9 F Em7 Dm7
Unison
In my bless-ed Lord I see. All that thrills my
61
G7 C Csus/D C/E Fm Fm2 Fm

fff
Divisi
soul is Je - sus. All that
fff
Divisi
Cm/E♭
Csus/D♭
D♭7♭5
C
65
thrills my soul is Je -
65
Fm
Fm2
Fm
fff
Cm/E♭
Csus/D♭
D♭7♭5
rit.
(6)
sus!
Je - sus!
C
G♭/C
C
G♭/C
A♭/C
N.C.
C
rit.

The Joy of the Lord

The Joy of the Lord
Rejoice, the Lord Is King
Rejoice in the Lord Always
Joyful, Joyful, We Adore Thee

Arranged by Don Marsh

*Words and Music by Twila Paris.

will be my strength, I will not fal - ter,
E♭2(no 3rd)
E♭sus E♭
13
I will not faint. He is my shep - herd, I
E♭sus/F E♭M7 A♭M7 B♭sus B♭ Cm B♭/C Cm Cm/B♭ B♭ Cm/B♭
13
CD: 54
am not a - fraid, The joy of the Lord is my
A♭M7 Fm/A♭ A♭ E♭2/G E♭/G Fm9 A♭M7 A♭M7/B♭ B♭7 A♭2/B♭

f
17
Divisi
strength. The joy of the Lord, the
Divisi f
Bb sus / Eb
Bb sus / Ab
Bb sus / G
Bb sus / F
Bb sus / G
17
AbM7
f
joy of the Lord, The joy of the Lord is my
Eb2 / G
Fm9
Fm7
AbM7 / Bb
Fm7 / Bb
21
strength. The joy of the Lord, the
Eb
Eb sus / F
Eb / G
B°
Cm
21
AbM7

CD: 55
joy of the Lord, The joy of the Lord is my
E♭ E♭2 4/F E♭ Cm7 Fm9 Fm7 A♭M7 Fm7/B♭
Unison
25
strength.
The joy of the Lord
Joy,
Unison
E♭ B♭/C C7 F Gm/F F
will be my strength,
my strength,
He will up - hold me
FM7 Gm/F F Gm/E F/E Gm/D Dm7

Divisi
29
all of my days.
I am sur-round - ed by
Gm7
F/G
C sus
C
Dm
Dm/C
CD: 56
Unison
mer - cy and grace,
The joy of the Lord is my
B♭M7
B♭6
F/A
Gm9
B♭M7/C
C7
33
*"Rejoice, the Lord Is King"
strength.
Re - joice, the Lord is
D♭
A♭sus/D♭
A♭
D♭/C

Divisi
King; Your Lord and King a - dore! Re -
Re -
Divisi
Unison
B♭m B♭m/A♭ D♭M7/A♭ G♭ D♭/F D♭sus/E♭ D♭ A♭2/C A♭/C A♭sus/B♭ A♭
37
joice, give thanks, and sing, And tri - umph ev - er -
joice and sing,
37
D♭ B♭m E♭ Cm D♭ A♭/E♭ E♭sus E♭
41
more. Lift up your heart; Lift
Divisi
A♭ Fm7 D♭/F
41
G♭2 G♭ F7sus F7 B♭m2 B♭m Fm7 B♭m

*Words from Philippians 4:4; Music, Anonymous. Arr.

Divisi
joice in the Lord al - ways, a - gain I say, re - joice. Re
Divisi
F2
C
F
F2
53
Soprano
joice, re - joice, a - gain I say, re - joice. Re -
Alto
joice in the Lord al - ways, a - gain I say, re - joice. Re -
Tenor
joice in the Lord al - ways, a - gain I say, re - joice. Re -
Bass
joice in the Lord al - ways, a - gain I say, re - joice. Re -
53
F
C7sus
C7
F
F
E

joice, re - joice, a - gain I say, re - joice.
joice in the Lord al - ways, a - gain I say, re - joice. Re -
joice, re - joice, a - gain I say, re - joice. Re -
joice in the Lord al - ways, a - gain I say, re - joice. Re -
Dm7 Am7 Gm7 C9 F
57
Re - joice, I say, re - joice.
joice, re - joice, a - gain I say, re - joice. Re -
joice, re - joice, a - gain I say, re - joice.
joice in the Lord al - ways, a - gain I say, re - joice. Re -
F/E Dm9 Gm7 C9 F F9/6

Re - joice, a - gain I say, re - joice.
joice, re - joice, a - gain I say, re - joice.
Re - joice, a - gain I say, re - joice. Re -
joice, re - joice, a - gain I say, re - joice. Re -
Dm7 Am7 Gm7 C9 F
61
Re - joice, I say, re - joice.
I say, re - joice, I say, re - joice.
joice, re - joice, a - gain I say, re - joice. Re -
joice, re - joice, a - gain I say, re - joice. Re -
61
F2 C/F Bb2/F C/F F2

*Words by Henry van Dyke; Music by Ludwig van Beethoven. Arr.

70
Hearts un - fold like flow'rs be - fore Thee,
C sus
C 7 sus
70
N.C.
Open - ing to the sun a - bove.
The
F2/C
C
F
C 7 sus
B♭2/C
73
joy of the Lord will be my strength,
73
F
Gm/F
F
Gm/F
F

I will not waiv - er, walk - ing by faith;
F Gm/F F B♭/F F B♭/F F C
77
CD: 59
Unison
He will be strong to de - liv - er me safe, The
Unison
Dm C/D Dm Dm/C C Dm/C B♭M7 Gm/B♭ B♭ F/A
Divisi
joy of the Lord is my strength. The
Divisi
Gm9 Gm7 B♭M7/C Gm7/C F B♭/F C/F F F2/A

81
A few voices
Joy of the Lord, joy of the
joy of the Lord, the joy of the Lord, The
81 B♭M7
F2/A
Lord, The Lord is my strength, my strength.
joy of the Lord is my strength. The
Gm9 Gm7 B♭M7/C Gm7/C
F Fsus/G F/A C♯° Dm

85
Joy of the Lord, joy of the
joy of the Lord, the joy of the Lord, The
85
B♭M7
F F4/2 F Dm7
Lord, The Lord is my strength.
joy of the Lord is my strength. The
Gm9 Gm7 B♭M7/C Gm7/C
F Gm/F F C/D Dm7

89
joy of the Lord is my strength!
Gm9 Gm7 B♭M7/C C13
C sus/F C sus/G C sus/A
C sus/B♭ C sus/A F sus/G
ff
Joy of the Lord!
Joy of the Lord!
F sus/G
N.C.
C sus/B♭ C sus/A F sus/G F